Worship Audit

Making Good Worship Better

Mark Earey
PRAXIS National Education Officer

GROVE BOOKS LIMITED
RIDLEY HALL RD, CAMBRIDGE CB3 9HU

Contents

Acknowledgements

I would like to thank the members of the Group for Renewal of Worship (GROW) who have been gracious in encouragement and honest enough to help me to improve what is presented here. I am also grateful to the Liturgical Committee of Leicester Diocese (under its then Chairman, David Silk) who first encouraged me to work on the approach outlined here (and then became the guinea pigs when it came to trying it out!), and to the Coventry Diocesan Liturgical Group, whose own Worship Audit material gave me much needed ideas about where to begin with the 'process' and the questionnaire.

Special thanks are also due to Michael Vasey, who first encouraged me to write this booklet, to Charles Prest, who helped to improve the structure, to the people of Christ the King, who have endured their minister going on about the theological principles involved, and above all, to Alison, my own Worship Auditor.

The Cover Illustration is by Kim Sewell

First Impression July 1995
Reprinted January 1998
ISSN 0144-1728
ISBN 1 85174 294 8

1
Introduction

A small group of people leave the warm interior of the church building, shaking hands earnestly with the vicar on their way out, and bracing themselves for the biting wind that blows round the corner of the tower. Behind them they hear footsteps approaching hurriedly and a voice asks, 'What did you think of the service tonight?' What happens in the split seconds that follow, as they first consider and then articulate their thoughts, is 'worship audit.'

Similar conversations happen in churches of every denomination up and down the country (and indeed all over the world) every week, and though the particular phrases and ways of asking and answering the question will vary according to the sort of church and the usual style of worship, the principle is the same—*worship can be evaluated.*

However, these conversations rarely result in any *change* in the worship offered the following week, unless one of the participants is the minister, or leads the worship group—and even then only if they are extremely secure and able to receive criticism and respond to it creatively. This is because such evaluation is primarily between individuals and made on the basis of individual criteria, usually to do with personal preferences for styles of music, dress and ceremonial.

So the evaluation (or 'auditing') of worship already happens. The blossoming interest in official schemes of 'worship audit' (or 'worship review') is the result of a desire to put this informal evaluation onto a firmer footing—to systematize this personal process so that it becomes a *conscious* activity of a wider group of people, which can then be used to improve the worship.

It may be wise at this stage to say a word about liturgical consultancy. Liturgical consultancy and worship audit are basically about the same thing: improvement in worship. The only difference is that they tend to come at it from different angles. Liturgical consultancy, which is also an area attracting a lot of interest in the church, is a part of worship audit. Worship audit can take place without consultancy, but it will be weaker for it. Liturgical consultancy, likewise, is of little use without a context in which the worshippers themselves want to think hard about the worship they are offering. This booklet comes from the worship audit angle and looks from the perspective of the worshippers, who, as part of their desire to improve their worship, may enlist the help of some 'consultant.' Liturgical consultancy tends to look at the situation from the perspective of the consultants who are considering ways of helping and advising the worshipping community.

The aim of this booklet is not to be the last word on the subject, but to draw together some of the strands of what is already happening and to suggest ways of broadening the criteria of assessment, remembering chiefly whose opinion matters above all others—God's!

2

What is Worship?

A Slippery Word

I remember a journal (*Expository Times*, I think) once running a series on 'Slippery Words.' I soon discovered that there are a lot of slippery words in regular use in the Christian church—words that everyone uses, but of which few people could give a coherent definition. 'Worship' is one of them. It is such an integral part of most Christians' lives that we *think* we know what we are talking about, when often we do not. Or, rather, we know what *we* mean—the trouble comes when we have to talk to someone else whose understanding is different!

For the purposes of this booklet I shall assume that we are talking about *corporate* worship, rather than private devotions. This is not because one is more truly 'worship' than the other, but because it is the nature of corporate worship as *public* and involving many different people that raises the issues I hope to address.

Definitions

The difficulty of coming to an agreement about what worship is does not stop people trying! It is certainly one of the bonuses of worship audit that it can lead people to think not only about what we do in worship, but also about *why* we do it and what we are *aiming* at in the first place. Attempted explanations come in all shapes and sizes, from the magisterial attempt by William Temple:

'To worship is to quicken the conscience by the holiness of God,

to feed the mind with the truth of God,

to purge the imagination by the beauty of God,

to open the heart to the love of God,

to devote the will to the purpose of God.'

to the rather less sublime:

'God's people being happy together upwards.'

This is a definition I remember being given very early on in my Christian life! I am unsure who first coined this, and might quibble with the 'happy,' and the topological reference to God. If it is amended to, 'God's people *being* together Godwards,' it makes a pretty good starting point for understanding the Sunday assembly of the church. Evelyn Underhill puts it like this:

'Worship, in all its grades and kinds, is the response of the creature to the Creator.'[1]

Here worship is seen as a natural mode of relationship, in the same way that friendship might be the natural mode between peers. However, worship *per se* does not have to include the idea of the divine, let alone a Creator. The word can

---

1   Evelyn Underhill, *Worship* (Nisbet & Co. 1936) p 3.

be used of relationship between humans, and though most grooms today balk at the idea of worshipping their bride just as much as she at the idea of obeying him, the reality of humans worshipping other humans is there on the walls of teenagers' rooms—and not just teenagers'!

The idea is taken further and made more reciprocal in the preface to the Methodist hymnbook, *Hymns and Psalms*, where worship is described as 'God's approach to us and our approach to God.'[2]

As if this were not enough, there has been some debate (among evangelicals in particular) about whether what most Christians do together on a Sunday is worship *at all* in a New Testament sense[3]—after all, does not the New Testament stress that the whole of our lives are a sacrifice offered to God in worship,[4] and that the fulfilment of temple, altar, priesthood and so on is to be found in Jesus himself?[5] Worship can then be defined as:

'...our engagement with God through faith in Jesus Christ and what he has done for us.'[6]

This is wide ranging indeed, and pretty well makes the whole of our Christian life worship. This leaves the Sunday meeting essentially to be about edification and education for the Christian life.[7] However, if worship is about the whole of our lives, then that certainly does not *exclude* the gathering of believers, for God takes pleasure in the praises of his people as well as in their obedient lives, and believers edify one another because that is what pleases God.[8] And if some Christians have been somewhat suspicious of an emphasis on the transcendent and numinous in public worship, there is now a new willingness to think in terms of the special presence of God among his people when they meet together, and among many there is an expectation that we should be able to sense and experience that presence. This is especially true among those influenced by the charismatic movement. In his recent book Pete Ward has a chapter entitled 'Meeting God in Worship.' He comments:

'Young people need to experience the presence of God...I am recommending an approach to evangelism that is based heavily on a sense of the presence of God...This experiential aspect of Christianity is most frequently seen in the

---

2 (*Hymns and Psalms*, Methodist Publishing House,1983, p vii). Graham Kendrick echoes this: 'Worship is God's enjoyment of us and our enjoyment of him.' (*Worship*, Kingsway, 1984, p 22).

3 See I Howard Marshall's essay *How far did the early Christians worship God?* in Churchman 99 (1985) p 216-299, or his article 'New Testament Worship' in JG Davies (ed) *A New Dictionary of Liturgy and Worship* (SCM, 1986).

4 As per Romans 12.1ff, where it is worth noting that verse 1 says, 'offer your bodies [plural] as a living sacrifice [singular]' stressing the corporate nature of what Paul is urging.

5 This is helpfully spelt out by David Peterson in his chapter on 'Worship in the New Testament' in Donald Carson (ed), *Worship: Adoration and Action* (World Evangelical Fellowship, 1993), especially p 71ff.

6 David Peterson, *ibid*, p 52.

7 The question of how much the Christian weekly gathering is about God's address to us and our response to God, and how much about our mutual edification as believers, is a live one. The issue is tackled in the 1988 Report to Methodist Conference of the Commission on Worship *Let the People Worship* paras 44-56 where a balance is advocated.

8 This is the line of argument taken by Donald Carson, *op cit* p 16. See also p 52.

presence of God amongst us when we worship.'[9]

Compare this with the Methodist Report:

'This presence is not dependent on our ability to sense it. God, thankfully is present whether we are aware of him or not...in every aspect of our daily life. However, worship is one of the appointed meeting places, where God has promised to be present.'[10]

At its most basic then, it is natural for us as Christians to gather together—we are family, after all, and even families that do not get on gather sometimes! And when we do gather, it is natural for us to express in word and action what it is that makes us belong to one another. That expression naturally includes ascribing 'worth' to the one who created and redeemed us and brought us together. Here we have come to the root of the English word: 'worship' is worth-ship. In Christian terms this means recentring our lives and our priorities by focussing on the King and his Kingdom. This is the natural activity of those in heaven who sing continually,

'You are *worthy*, our Lord and God,
to receive glory and honour and power,
for you created all things,
and by your will they existed and were created.
Worthy is the Lamb that was slain...' (Rev 4.11 and 5.12)

---

9 *Worship and Youth Culture* (Marshall Pickering. 1993) p 23f.
10 1988 Report to Methodist Conference of the Commission on Worship *Let the People Worship* para 28.

3
Why Worship Audit?

We tend to associate detailed instructions about the mechanics of an act of worship with the *Old* Testament, but the New Testament also makes it clear that there are appropriate and inappropriate ways of behaving when the church meets.[11]

Back in the 'good old days' in the Church of England, worship was relatively straightforward, because worship *was* the Book of Common Prayer (give or take). It is a combination of the liturgical and charismatic renewals (and the variety of liturgical material that has recently come on the scene) which has caused the issue to become such a live one.[12] Of course there were always those (of all shades of church tradition) who would 'stretch' the rubrics and the text of the BCP, and there was always room for variety and improvement in the choice of music and hymns, the preaching, the prayers and so on. But what the ASB did, as did its immediate predecessors to a certain extent, was to enshrine variety—and therefore the act of *choice* and *decision*—in the text and rubrics of the service itself.[13] Liturgical flexibility has moved on in leaps and bounds since those heady days,[14] but as well as freedom it has brought tremendous responsibility to those who lead Anglican worship, because the quality of the worship depends much more on them and on the decisions they make, either during the service or at the word processor in their study beforehand. To put it another way, it has meant making the move from *taking a service* (or reading the service) to *leading worship*—a move which, it has to be said, many have not made easily!

The formation of *Praxis* has been just one of the results of people taking this change seriously.[15] Improving people's knowledge of what is available in terms of texts, tightening up their technical skills and helping their theological reflection are all useful things. But where the rubber hits the road is back home in the parish church, or hospital or prison chapel, and that is where the decisions have to be made about what is appropriate worship for *these* people at *this* time in *this* place. And that depends as much on them and on the building, the atmosphere, the traditions of that church and so on as it does on whether they are using an

---

11 See for instance, 1 Corinthians 11 and 14, and James 2.1-4.

12 Incidentally, it is interesting to note the moves in the opposite direction by other denominations over the same period to provide more written texts for worship (though without the Anglican emphasis on conformity). Note also the recent appearance in the Spring Harvest songbooks of liturgical material which they call, rather prosaically, 'Words for Worship.'

13 With its black (compulsory) and blue (optional) section numbers, 'other suitable words' and alternative Eucharistic Prayers, confession, and forms of intercession.

14 *Lent, Holy Week, Easter; Patterns for Worship; Promise of His Glory,* not to mention the recently authorised *Service of the Word.*

15 *Praxis* is a joint venture of the Liturgical Commission, Alcuin Club and GROW to put liturgical training on the agenda of clergy and lay folk alike by organising training events and day conferences (mainly in London) and by supporting and encouraging similar events organised regionally.

appropriate seasonal introduction to the confession.

What is more, it is a golden rule of the professional training world that training is useless without *evaluation*—something which the Church of England is only slowly coming to terms with.[16] But evaluation should lead to action. Worship audit should cause some churches to change established patterns, but in a thought-out way, which hopefully will mean less chance of those changes having to be reversed shortly afterwards.

For others, it will be a good chance to stop and consider changes that have already been made, or are planned, and to check what has been, or may be, lost. It is especially important that those who are in the position to make changes to the worship of a church do take stock in this public way, which forces them to consider the views of the other worshippers. Though we need to have an eye to the outsider, it is easy to use this as an excuse and to forget that we have to plan and lead worship for the congregation we *have* got, not just the congregation we *wish* we had! Often those at the front ignore, or are simply out of touch with, the congregation they have. Or they base their decisions on caricatures of the people in the pews. Of course, 'market forces' cannot be allowed to rule decisions about worship, but consultation is essential if decisions for change are not to be *unnecessarily* destructive.[17]

There will almost always be a tension here. There is a need for bold prophetic leadership which is willing to be unpopular where change is needed. But a true desire to change worship with mission in mind will involve a thorough and *realistic* understanding of the prevailing non-church cultures in the church's area.

16 For instance. in the area of Clergy Appraisal. and of Parish or Mission Audit.
17 For more on managing change. see Trevor Lloyd. *Introducing Liturgical Change* (Grove Worship Series No.87) and Administry's Project Resource Paper 87.6 *Changed for Life - managing change without destructive conflict.*

4
What is Worship Audit?

In short, worship audit is a way of describing a systematic attempt to evaluate the quality of the corporate worship which we offer to God. Here we are immediately in trouble, of course, because the word 'quality' has become an extremely loaded one in the area of worship, and particularly music.

Three Points of View

I want to suggest that worship audit, if done properly, should evaluate the worship on the basis of three different perspectives:

1. **What does *God* think of it?**
   (Does this worship achieve its aim of ascribing 'worth' to God?)

2. **What do *we* think of it?**
   (Does this worship help all those who have come to the service to be able to offer their worship together?)

3. **What do *they* think about it?**
   (Are there some things about the way we worship together which make it harder than it need be for new people to join us in worship?)

The third of these is a perspective we are being encouraged to consider more and more in this Decade of Evangelism when the church service is being described as the church's shop window. But the idea that there are likely to be unbelievers in the meeting of the church (and that we should be aware of what they might think of what is going on!) goes back to St Paul (1 Cor 14.23-25).

The second perspective is the one we most naturally tend to, with our assessment of whether 'the worship was any good this evening,' or whether 'I enjoyed the service this morning.' A major step forward is to acknowledge that the others present are integral, and not merely incidental, to the event of corporate worship, and therefore their needs and preferences matter. From there it is another step to bring in considerations other than enjoyment, such as 'duty'.[18] But even this is not enough. Worship should be for God's pleasure and our benefit, but we often think of it the other way around. This brings us to the first of the three perspectives above.

---

18 'It is not only right, it is our duty and our joy' as ASB Rite A puts it in the First Eucharistic Prayer. The concept of duty is not a popular one today, particularly among those who have recently been released from what they have experienced as the dead hand of worship which was duty and not much else, into worship which is lively and 'spirit-filled' and touches the emotions and spirit as well as the head.

Worship considered from the perspective of God's pleasure is the hardest to assess and the most likely to cause friction. We are not God, and anyone who dares to speak must, to a certain extent, risk speaking for God. And yet it surely is the key to understanding whether what we do when we come together as the Church is actually worth anything at all, or whether we might as well give up and go home and watch the Morning Service on the television instead—which, of course, many people do. To try to see our worship from God's perspective is no easy task and will involve a lot of theological work which we can only begin here. But it is something that the Old Testament prophets were not afraid to do, and in our own day it should not be avoided.

For the Leader

For the leader there are particular challenges to be faced at the outset of worship audit. By the very nature of the exercise it is likely to bring to the surface, along with much that is constructive and positive, many negative reactions and fears in the congregation. These can find their response in a defensive attitude on the part of the leader or leaders.

Two areas are particularly going to need addressing. First is the way you lead—your own particular style and preferences when you lead acts of worship. Second is the issue of pastoral management—the way things to do with worship get organized, who decides what services you have, how rotas are produced, who determines who does what when, who chooses music and so on.

There is too much to address it all here, but it is as well to be aware of the issues in advance and perhaps to do a little personal audit of one's own style and theology of leading worship.[19]

Self-assessment and Consultancy

In practice worship audit, like the best mission audit, is *self-assessment* according to 'self-determined' criteria, but with the help and advice of an outside consultant.[20] In the Anglican set-up this might well be a member of the Diocesan Worship or Liturgical Committee, but it would not need to be. It could usefully be a person from a nearby church which has already undergone a worship audit, or simply someone known and respected who has some idea of the issues involved in reviewing worship. This use of an outside consultant is the part of worship audit which it is most tempting to miss out, but it is crucial to its success.

The consultant is the third point of an audit triangle. The first point is us and our experience of the acts of worship we already have. The second is the Bible

---

19 Colin Buchanan's *Leading worship* (Grove Worship series no.76) has good thought-provoking theological background as well as very practical tips. More recently, Paul James's *Liturgical Presidency* (Alcuin/GROW Liturgical Study 24) is strong on description and issues of training for leading worship (mainly Eucharistic worship), but perhaps weaker and at times a bit restrictive when dealing with what worship leading should be like.

20 Though hopefully, 'self-determined' not in an individualistic sense, but only in the sense of *priorities* for this time and place determined from a biblical and theological foundation.

and the third is the consultant, who represents the Christian tradition across time and place who comes to help us wrestle with the theology and experience of worship.

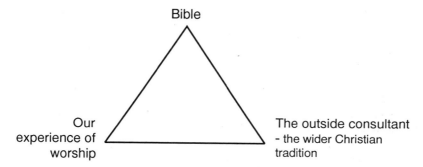

I would suggest two criteria for choosing an outside consultant (or consultants):[21]

1. Someone whom people in the church, and especially on the audit team, will trust;
2. Someone with a different perspective, ideally from a different church tradition, who will be able to spot the unspoken assumptions of the church, and be able to challenge them, but who will do so from a position of sympathy and understanding of those assumptions.

As well as giving an 'outsider's' theological critique, the consultant can also give a genuine report of how your worship feels to an newcomer who comes to your church for the first time. All those things that you and your regulars take for granted will be spotted by such an 'outsider,' which could save you missing vital clues as to how to improve your worship. Even better of course is to enlist the help of genuine visitors as well. You could perhaps devise a simple questionnaire which focuses on the things a visitor might notice, and ask members of the congregation to give it to family and friends who come to stay and who come to worship with them as part of that stay. Better still if some of those visitors are not Christians or regular worshippers at any church.

---

21 From the point of view of dioceses and other bodies trying to establish a team of such consultants, there are important issues surrounding their training—most obviously, that they should have some.

5
How Do We Do Worship Audit?

Some dioceses now have established procedures for carrying out worship audit, with flexibility so that it can 'fit' the particular situation and needs of individual churches. Most will follow the sort of pattern set out below, or something similar.

Stage 1: Decision
The PCC with the vicar (or equivalent group in a non-parish context), must decide whether or not to undertake a worship audit and when it is to be done. The whole process will take several months. You may decide to invite a member of the diocesan Liturgical Committee, or someone from a church which has already undertaken a worship audit, to explain what is involved first. It may be that a full audit is too much to take on. In that case, there is a lot to be said for starting small—perhaps an audit of all-age or 'family' services, or of the worship provision on Sunday evenings?

The audit is coordinated and carried out by a team, usually made up of:
- those responsible for regular planning and leading of worship —clergy, readers, organist, choir or music group leader, worship committee members;
- some ordinary members of the congregation as 'consumers' (including at least some PCC members);
- and someone else from 'outside' whom you have invited to share in the process as a consultant (perhaps a member of the diocesan Liturgical Committee).

The dates and times of two main services which will be 'audited' should be agreed. These should avoid as much as possible 'one-off' special services and concentrate on the *normal* worship pattern of *most* of the congregation. Two services is suggested so as to give a more balanced view than would be possible by just considering one service. You could of course use more than two services. The more you consider the better the results are likely to be, but the more work it will involve.

Stage 2: Audit of Two Main Services
One of the most obvious ways of discovering the views of the worshippers is to use some form of questionnaire and most diocesan schemes use one. An example is given in the centre pages of this booklet, but most churches will probably want to produce their own, in order to tailor it to their own needs.

If a questionnaire is used, every member of the congregation at two services is given a questionnaire, which they are asked to complete after the service—preferably straight away and not at home afterwards. Teenage children can be given copies of the questionnaire. The audit team should consult with children's leaders to think about the best ways of gaining feedback from younger children.

Questionnaires are by no means the only (or the best) way of considering the worship from the perspective of the worshippers. For fuller discussion on this see

The Question of Worship

This questionnaire is designed to help this church to assess its worship and to see if there are areas which need improving. It would be a great help if you could answer these questions.

Where there are boxes, please tick the most appropriate one. Some questions require you to give an answer on a scale from 1 to 10 (where **10 is the best** and 1 is the worst) - please put a ring round the number that best reflects your feelings.

What was the Date and Time of this Service?

SECTION A Tell us a bit about yourself:

A.1 Which of the following best sums you up?

1 ☐ I am here for worship most Sundays

2 ☐ I come quite often (say, between 10 and 20 times a year)

3 ☐ I come occasionally (less than 10 times a year)

4 ☐ This is a special visit (perhaps because of a Baptism or Wedding Banns, or because of a recent bereavement or you are visiting relatives)

5 ☐ Other...

A.2 If you are a regular worshipper (1 above), then how long have you been worshipping here?

1 ☐   less than a year

2 ☐   1-5 years

3 ☐   5-10 years

4 ☐   more than 10 years

A.3 Do you regularly worship at another church?   ☐ Yes   ☐ No

A.4 Which of these age groups do you fit into?
1 ☐ 0-12   2 ☐ 13-20   3 ☐ 21-40
4 ☐ 41-60   5 ☐ 60+

A.5 Are you,
☐ Female
☐ Male

SECTION B   Before the service started...

B.1 How good did you feel the welcome was when you arrived?

1   2   3   4   5   6   7   8   9   10

B.2 How helpful did you find the 'atmosphere' in church before the service?

1   2   3   4   5   6   7   8   9   10

B.3 Do you have any other comments to make about things before the service, or suggestions for improvement?

SECTION C   During the Service....

C.1 How easy did you find the service book or leaflets to use and follow?

1   2   3   4   5   6   7   8   9   10

C.2 Was the print large enough for you to read?   ❑ Yes   ❑ No

C.3 Did you have any other problems with seeing or hearing during the service? If so, what particularly?

C.4 How helpful and clear was the leadership of the service?

1   2   3   4   5   6   7   8   9   10

C.5 How well did the service seem to 'hang together' (give a high score if it felt good, and a low one if it felt a bit disconnected)

1   2   3   4   5   6   7   8   9   10

C.6 How helpful did you find any symbolism and ceremonial used?

1   2   3   4   5   6   7   8   9   10

C.7 Do you have any other comments about things in this section?

SECTION D Music

D.1 How well do you feel the music fitted with the rest of what went on in the service?

1   2   3   4   5   6   7   8   9   10

D.2 How happy were you with the mix of styles of music (eg. traditional and modern)?

1   2   3   4   5   6   7   8   9   10

D.3 Was any of the music unfamiliar to you?   ❏ Yes   ❏ No

D.4 How well did the music help you to praise or adore God?

1   2   3   4   5   6   7   8   9   10

D.5 Any other comment about the music?

SECTION E Sermon, readings and prayers

E.1 How understandable and clear did you find the sermon/talk?

1   2   3   4   5   6   7   8   9   10

E.2 How challenging or thought-provoking did you find the sermon/talk?

1   2   3   4   5   6   7   8   9   10

E.3 How helpful was the way the Bible reading was introduced and read?

1   2   3   4   5   6   7   8   9   10

E.4 How helpful did you find the intercessions (prayers)?

1   2   3   4   5   6   7   8   9   10

E.5 How helpful was the service for giving you silence to use for yourself (perhaps a chance for you to do your own praying and reflecting after the readings, during the prayers, or after communion)?

1   2   3   4   5   6   7   8   9   10

E.6 Do you have any comments to make about the sermon, bible reading/s, intercessions (prayers) or use of silence?

E.7 How well did you feel that the worship was connected to your daily life (perhaps by things that were said in the sermon, or mentioned in the prayers)?

1   2   3   4   5   6   7   8   9   10

E.8 Did you feel part of the worship, or did any aspects make you feel excluded, unwelcome, awkward, stupid, or second-class?

If you have time, you may like to think about the following:

F.1 What does 'reverence' mean to you?

F.2 Think about the other people who were present. Obviously not everyone might feel the same about the worship as you did. Do you think there are any particular things about which others would have felt quite differently to you?

F.3 Do your home circumstances allow you to have your own private prayer/devotions on a regular basis (if you wanted to)?

❏ Yes

❏ No

❏ Yes - but I find it hard to know how to use such time.

chapter 7 below. One member of the audit team takes the completed question-naires, with conclusions and views obtained from other forms of consultation, to do an analysis of the results, collating statistics and summarizing comments.

Stage 3: Worship Audit Team Discussions

First, using the ideas from chapter 6 of this booklet (or some other starting point) as a basis, there should first be a discussion to settle the underlying 'theo-logical' assumptions which will guide the evaluation of the worship and which will determine norms and aims for future development.

Before the meeting, each member of the team should have a copy of the col-lated results of the questionnaire (or, in the case of a small congregation, have seen all the completed questionnaires) and some form of written material about a theological framework for the assessment of the results.

It would help if at least some of the team have read *In Tune With Heaven* , the report of the Archbishops' Commission on Church Music, and all members would benefit from having copies of its final recommendations in chapter 30. There may need to be two or more meetings of the team at this stage, as the question of music in worship alone is often an extremely significant one, needing careful thought.

The team should then go through the sections of the questionnaire and consider the issues raised. The input of the outside consultant and the 'coaching' questions suggested in chapter 8 of this booklet will be of particular help at this stage. Where there is a consensus in the questionnaires on any aspects of worship, these should be given particular attention. The team should appoint a secretary to prepare a preliminary report based on these discussions before the final meeting.

Stage 4: Final Meeting—Conclusions and Recommendations

Each member of the team should have a copy of the preliminary report of discussions and the secretary should also distribute a table of the current monthly pattern of services. The secretary's report should be discussed and a shorter over-all evaluation of the strengths and weaknesses in the worship and should be agreed. The team should then determine priorities and make recommendations for fu-ture development. They might consider the following questions:
1. Does the range of services meet the varying needs of those who might share in the life of the congregation—those who as yet do *not* as well as those who do?
2. Has the pattern of services and the level of attendance at them changed in recent years? What might be the reasons?
3. After considering the results of the worship audit, what should be our priori-ties for the future long term development of our public worship?
4. What short term action might be appropriate in the light of any recent changes to the pattern of worship services or to the levels of attendance?

The team presents its overall evaluation and recommendations to the Church Council (or equivalent) for them to consider what action to take. An important part of this action will be communicating the results of the questionnaire and the audit to the congregation and explaining any changes which are to result.

6
What Does God Think of Our Worship?

Each worship audit team will want to be clear about its own agreed basis before it begins to assess strengths and weaknesses in the worship. Otherwise one person's idea of a strength will be another's idea of a weakness, simply because they are each working on different assumptions of what worship is all about. This should be part of the discussion at stage 3. There is a need for realism here. A watertight and totally unanimous definition of worship is not likely, nor is it needed. What is needed is a theological framework to help to focus the Team's mind as it works through the questionnaires, and the preferences and views of its own members.

Below are some biblical criteria which are applicable. This is by no means an attempt to set out a complete theology of worship, nor to give an outline survey of all that the Bible has to say on worship.[22] The audit team will need to discuss, and probably add to, the three principles outlined here. These are given to indicate how theology may be related to practise.

Sacrifice

This is a word which we perhaps most immediately apply to Old Testament worship, with its elaborate instructions about offerings and Temple furniture. But in the New Testament it is there as a principle for the whole of our Christian lives. It is there in Jesus' warning that followers of his must lay down their own lives and take up their crosses (Mark 8.34f) and Paul uses similar imagery in Romans 12.1, urging his readers to offer the whole of their lives as a sacrifice, which is the worship God requires.

Using the principle that what applies in the whole of our lives applies equally when we meet as the church, it is worth asking ourselves whether our worship is designed for our own convenience or whether it 'costs' us? For instance, is our worship the place where we come to indulge ourselves spiritually, psychologically, aesthetically or emotionally? Are we 'offering the Lord that which costs us nothing' (2 sam 24.24)? There is, of course, a big place in the Old Testament for the worshipper to enjoy the benefit of their 'offering' to the Lord in feasting and eating together,[23] but this is always only half the story. Is our corporate worship the *focus* of the offering of our whole selves and lives (Romans 12.1ff), or a *replacement* for it? Are we willing to sacrifice our preferences for the sake of others who, perhaps through age, or through having come to faith with no church background, may be less able to adapt?

---

22 For excellent surveys of worship in the Old and New Testaments see the chapters by Yoshiaki Hattori and David Peterson respectively in Donald Carson (ed) *op cit.*

23 1 Samuel 1.1-18 for instance records such a festival, where the worshippers ate together as part of their worship, using a portion of the peace offering they had brought.

Integrity

This is the way we might sum up the message of the Old Testament prophets—Micah 6, Amos 5, and Isaiah 66 for example—and it raises questions of ethics *within* corporate worship.[24]

The Prophets' message is that no matter how beautiful our services are, God is not pleased if what we sing and say with our mouths has no relation to the way we live our lives (or the way we run our church) when we are not in the worshipping assembly. Or, to put it another way, God desires the love of our *hearts* which is focussed in corporate worship and lived out in the everyday.

We are perhaps familiar with the idea that our devotion and love for God must not be divorced from our moral behaviour. After all, that much is clear from the Ten Commandments. But while we sing of God's love for all, does our church life (or indeed, our very *act of worship* itself) scream 'injustice, hatred, unforgiveness, envy, bitterness, racism...'?[25]

In the New Testament the book of James has much to say about the evil of showing favouritism in the church meeting, which might inform our approach both to tramps and drunks at Christmas midnight communion, and to mayors and dignitaries at civic services, bishops' enthronements, and institution services! Similarly, the apostle Paul complains about divisions when believers come together as a church and about their greed and their impatience with one another (1 Cor 11.18). The relationships between worship leaders can have a profound (even if unconscious) effect on the worship. Where there is mistrust and rivalry between musicians, or between organist and vicar or music group, do we act to allow God to change things, or do we just ignore it and allow the worship to be poisoned by bad feeling and bitterness? These are very real issues in many churches today. And this is just to consider the question of internal integrity! Things look even more challenging when we begin to ask how the church is perceived in the wider community. Are we seen as those who are loving our enemies, bearing with others, considering others first?—or are we seen as heavy handed, privileged and judgmental?

Spirit and Truth

The rather enigmatic passage in John 4.19-26 is one of the keys to understanding worship from a New Testament perspective. It comes in the context of Jesus' conversation with the Samaritan woman at the well. She hopes to be let off the hook by talking about differences in worship practice. For her, true worship is

---

24 At one of the theological colleges in England, the Ethics tutor was once heard to say to the Liturgy tutor, 'What I teach is worship—what you teach is ecclesiastical group dynamics.'

25 I once knew of a parish church with a fine choral tradition and a superb choir which was open to men and boys only, ostensibly for musical and evangelistic purposes. There was an understandable sense of injustice expressed by girls who were involved in this church, not to mention a wonderful irony in the fact that women were not able to lead the singing of the Magnificat, the Song of Mary, at Evensong. The uninitiated might perhaps have deduced that, whilst God enjoyed the song when Mary sang it, he would have been much happier if Joseph had done so.

about which mountain to have the temple on. Jesus urges to her to see beyond the idea of God tied to one mountain or the other and to look for true worship which will be in 'Spirit and truth' (verse 21).

Is our worship too closely associated with a particular 'mountain,' or does it reflect the freedom and life of our God who refuses to be boxed in? Are we showing that there is more than one way to worship corporately?

In the wider context of John's gospel the Spirit is associated with the new life of the kingdom (John 3) and with truth (John 14-16). Does our worship show concern for the truth about God revealed in Christ (John 1.14): said, sung and implied? Would the casual visitor realise that our beliefs are trinitarian? Is there respect for the truths of the faith as they have been understood in previous generations and handed down, or do we give the impression that we think we have invented true Christianity in our own generation? At the same time, is there room for those for whom the Christian way is a recent new life and not a lifelong inheritance?

In the wider New Testament context (for example in 1 Cor 12-14), Spirit and truth may be seen as the balance between, on the one hand, everyone being able to make their contribution to the corporate worship because all have the Spirit (1 Cor 14.26) and on the other hand, everything being done in order, 'for God is a God of order...' (1 Cor 14.33).

How do we hold together the life of the Spirit and the truth of the gospel? As a youngster I was a bus-spotter, and so perhaps you will allow me to indulge myself in a 'transport' analogy.

There is a *'tram'* mentality to worship which stresses truth and order, but sometimes seemingly at the expense of Spirit and life. The rails fix the route. You always know where you are going, and different drivers make little difference, except that you might get there a bit faster or slower. Many people (particularly in the Anglican tradition, though not exclusively so) like their worship to be like that. Trams get their power from an outside source, via fixed rails or overhead cables. So for many people, the power of worship is mediated to them via tried and tested familiar forms; to hop off the rails is to grind to a halt. Trams are reliable but inflexible. If the road gets dug up, they cannot make a minor detour. New building and development can mean the end of them. Some folk are completely thrown by new services or songs, or changes to established patterns—sometimes so much so that they feel unable to worship at all in a church and go elsewhere or nowhere.

Motor buses on the other hand are supremely flexible. The route can be changed easily to accommodate minor road works and major new features. But this makes some passengers nervous. After all, you seem to be at the mercy of the driver, who might take you where you do not want to go, or at least via a route you were not expecting. Motor buses carry their own motive power, which (with regular fuelling) allows them to go where trams cannot. Many people in our churches today are looking for a flexible worship experience which will take them to different places—sometimes a different place every week, and certainly by a different route. Conscious of God's power in them, they do not feel the need to stick to well worn tracks. They can seem cavalier in their approach to tradition, and in their exciting journeys they seem in danger of missing much which is on their doorstep. Truth handed down seems to take a second place to experience and freedom.

Is there a middle way? *Trolley-buses* are currently enjoying a renaissance in transport circles. Running on tyres rather than rails, they have the advantage of flexibility when there is an obstruction in the road, or the need to change the route to accommodate a changed situation. Yet they take their power from over-head lines and so are not totally independent and at the mercy of the driver. Is this a possible way of understanding worship which is in Spirit and truth? What are your services most like?

Some Questions to Ask

At the conclusion of your discussions it might be worth trying to summarize where you have ended up. Bearing in mind all the biblical and other material, ask yourselves these questions:

- How are we defining 'corporate worship'?
- What is God's purpose for us as we gather on Sunday (as we understand it)?
- Is that purpose generally reflected in what we do and the way we do it?
- Are we working towards that purpose or against it?
- If we were to start from scratch, what would we do?
- What things from our heritage and tradition help us, and which hinder?
- Which parts of our heritage are we at liberty to change without reference to the wider church?[26]

---

26 Probably best to think in terms of things a bit less major than the ordination of women presbyters and the question of who should preside at the Holy Communion, which touch on exactly this question!

7

What Do 'We' Think of It and What Do 'They' Think of It?

The aim of the questionnaire, and other feedback from the congregation, is to give help and a wider perspective to the team in tackling the second and third areas of assessment given above—'What do *we* think of it?' and 'What do *they* think of it?'

It must be stressed that the questionnaire in the centre pages is simply a suggestion to give you ideas for questions you could include, and a starting point. It can be reproduced for local use (without copyright restriction) but in most cases it will need tailoring to particular churches and their needs.

For instance, the questions are mainly factual, or relate to how people experience the worship themselves. There is little that relates very closely to *particular* aspects of the theology of what we think we *ought* to be doing in worship. This is deliberate, and is to avoid prejudging the discussions and conclusions of individual audit Teams, and the priorities and terminology which are appropriate for their situation. At a detailed and technical level, churches may prefer to use a scale of 1-5, or 'Good-Poor' rather than 1-10.

It must be stressed that the results from the questionnaires (or other feedback) do not give the 'answers' as to what is right or wrong with the church's worship. They are simply a tool to help the audit team to discern the mind of the congregation and to consider these concerns in balance with the theological framework.

Questionnaires are difficult to construct well. If the questions are not carefully thought through the answers will be either useless, or they will simply confirm the prejudices of the writer as people will give the answer they think you want.[27]

In addition, questionnaires themselves have their limitations, no matter how carefully they are produced. The information gained from them is usually mainly 'raw' statistics which have to be carefully interpreted. The more opportunity there is for extended comment (rather than just tick boxes or rating from 1-10) the more subtlety there is, but results are then much harder to summarize in an easily digestible form. And, in many situations, a wordy questionnaire may not be the best way of getting the information required. The audit team should consider other methods, such as discussion groups after the service or using existing groups—home groups, women's fellowship, youth group, Boy's Brigade who come to Parade services, Mother's Union, parent and toddler groups—to encourage people to express an opinion. This could be used in conjunction with a questionnaire, or instead of one.

---

27 Administry's Project Resource paper 88:1 *Taking Stock* looks at how to audit various aspects of a church's life, and includes the use of questionnaires.

In most situations it will be important to allow people to express opinions in *more than one way*—in other words, not to rely on a questionnaire alone.[28] Discussion also enables people to engage with the theology, as well as their own likes and dislikes, in a similar way to the audit team.

The way a questionnaire is presented and explained to the church is crucial. It should be stressed that it is to *help* the church to help themselves, and is not an attempt by the diocese or anyone else to 'check up' on them. Explain that completed questionnaires are *not* used outside the local church, and that comments that people may make on them are confidential to the audit team. If the audit is part of a Diocesan scheme it may be that the diocesan Liturgical or Worship Committee may like to have some indication of the *general* results of the whole audit, and a list of what services of worship you currently offer (and what form they take) and any changes to your provision. Then they can build up a picture of what is happening around the diocese and so be better able to match their provision to the needs and situation at the grass roots. If so, this will need to be explained. It should be made clear that each questionnaire is anonymous, but that people may put their names on if they wish.

Where questionnaires are used, they are collected at the end of the service before people leave the church. People may wish to take them home to give further thought, but this is probably best discouraged for two reasons. First, there is the risk that fewer will actually be returned, because people never get round to filling it in once they get home, or they end up being away for several weeks, or they simply forget to hand it in. This reduces usefulness of the data collected because it does not give such a full picture.

Secondly, because in their reflection at home when the particular service in question is out of mind, the results you get may have more to do with general preferences or dislikes, or complaints which may stem from the distant past. Of course, a more general view will be valuable to the team and will certainly be the result if you also use discussion groups. But if particular individuals are pressing for more time to complete the questionnaire it is probably best to encourage them to complete it after the service with everyone else, and then to submit other thoughts, views, or comments to the team in the form of a letter, or to make sure their view is considered in a discussion group.

---

28 This is good psychology—in 'Myers-Briggs' terms it ensures that people with a preference for Extraversion (E) and/or Feeling (F) are heard (with apologies to those who are not familiar with the Myers-Briggs Type Indicator). For more information about the MBTI, see Isabel Briggs Myers, *Gifts Differing* (Consulting Psychologists Press, 1993), or one of the many other books on the market about personality type.

8

Suggested 'Coaching' Questions
to Help in Discussions

With the theological framework for assessment in mind the team will then need to turn to the specifics of the questionnaire and other forms of feedback from the worshippers, and the things brought up by them.[29]

The further questions and thoughts below are mainly intended to help the audit team in their discussions, but some of the ideas may usefully be used to open up discussion among other members of the congregation who meet to share opinions after (or instead of) using the questionnaire.

Not all these questions will be directly answerable from the questionnaires, nor are they meant to be. The questions here are meant to kick-start discussion and to highlight possible areas to consider *in the light of* the questionnaires, to tie discussion down. Some will be more relevant than others. There has been no attempt to raise every issue.

The structure of the questions below has been tied in to the sections and numbers of the questionnaire given in the centre pages, but they do not have to be used in conjunction with the questionnaire.

SECTION A (The people who were there during the worship)

- [A.1 & A.2] What proportion of the congregation has been worshipping here regularly for more than (say) 5 years? What effect will that have on the response to any proposed changes?
- [A.1] Do you have large numbers of visitors attending services, or people coming infrequently, and what considerations will their presence require? Why are they coming? Are they likely to be familiar with the way things happen in church?
- [A.4] Is any particular age range dominant? Why? So what?
- Are the elderly feeling (or being) marginalized? How easy is it for people to bring young children to the services? Is there somewhere a baby's nappy can be easily and comfortably changed for instance? Can you get to toilets without drawing attention to yourself?[30] If there are lots of children present, do they so dominate that other people find it impossible to concentrate at any

---

29 Another perspective, which there is not room to go into here, is the psychological perspective. The growth of interest in the Myers-Briggs Type Indicator and other measures of personality and temperament has shown that people's preferences and needs in the areas of spirituality and worship are determined by their psychology as well as their theology. This has big implications for those who plan and lead worship, for we tend to provide for others things that we find helpful ourselves.

30 I know of a church where a trip to the loo during the service means going to the churchwarden and get the key to another building—not something a visitor is likely to want to do twice!

time during the service. What about young people? Whether your church is being 'successful' in its work with young people or not, has it taken seriously the fact that since the late 1950s/early 1960s 'youth cultures' have existed, with often quite separate norms, values, art and music to the prevailing adult cultures? This is much more than a question of different *styles*—it is about the whole way the world is seen. Are your worship planners and preachers aware of changes in educational practice, stressing active participation and the questioning of assumptions? Have you considered that many young people no longer have social skills to equip them for any formal gatherings, let alone church services? You may want to devote much more time to the consideration of 'youth issues' as they relate to the *normal* worship of your church (as opposed to 'youth services' or the youth group).

- [A.5] Is there a dominance of male or female in the congregation, and is that reflected as much as possible in the 'up front' roles in the service? If not, is that because of thought out policy and decision, or are unspoken assumptions or prejudice affecting decisions about who does what?

SECTION B (Welcome and atmosphere)

- Most of us have assumptions about what the atmosphere in church before a service *should* be like. Is there a consensus in the church about what most people would like (for example: quiet for personal prayer, or inspiring songs led by a group), and is this possible (realistically) to enforce on others? Are there other ways of encouraging an element of stillness (or of joyful enthusiasm) *within* or *after* the service if people are unhappy about the atmosphere before the service?

- Is there always a last minute rush to get everything ready, and does that distract the congregation from their own preparation? Do the clergy and other leaders need to make sure they get a chance to pray and prepare unharrassed by last minute notices and people button-holing them about things which could wait until after the service?

- Is there an atmosphere of expectation—and if so, what are people expecting, and do they go away disappointed?!

- What about the general state of the church building? Inside, does it look tatty or tidy? Colourful or dull? Is there a beauty to it, even if a simple beauty? How does this affect the mood of worshippers?

SECTION C (During the service)

- [C.1] For regular worshippers using a familiar service the announcement of page numbers and so on can be a real distraction in worship. But for visitors it can be impossible to worship when one is constantly lost in an unfamiliar book. Is the amount of help given geared well to the needs of those who are actually there? Is the language used too 'churchy' to help newcomers?

- [C.2 & C.3] Are there other similar issues to be considered such as disabled access? Have you considered the needs of the partially-sighted in your provision of written material and size of print on OHP slides? Is there a loop system for those with hearing aids?

- [C.4] Leaders who are confused and confusing draw attention to themselves and are distracting. On the other hand, a service which always runs like clockwork can seem mechanical and inhuman. Are you erring to far in one direction or the other? Are there key moments in your worship where you need to avoid 'breaking the aura'? Is the slot for the 'notices' in the best place? Do you need the notices at all—is there another way to communicate the same information? If you have to have notices, would it be better to really make something of them in a creative way? For a start, who gives them?

- [C.5] Is there a sense of purpose as the worship proceeds and a shape to the service, or does it all feel rather aimless and dull? Though a theme can be helpful to hold the service together, equally it can become rather limiting if followed slavishly. There may be good reason for not stressing the theme of a particular week, for instance in the course of a teaching series where it would be forcing things to relate the music to the theme of the sermon. Is there more *subtle* thematic linking (by allusion), as well as the more obvious and direct? More important than a 'theme' as such, is whether there is a coherence and structure to the service and a sense of progressing through it, or whether it feels like a series of disconnected items.

- [C.6] Is the symbolism which is part of your regular worship living and clear?[31] If it has to be explained at length to a newcomer then it is probably not being very effective as symbol. Has it become stylized and unthinking? Does the worship experience engage body, mind and spirit?

SECTION D (Music)

- Is there a healthy balance between the spoken, sung/played, listening and silence in services? The team should use these questions in conjunction with the much fuller set of recommendations and issues raised in the Report of the Archbishops' Commission on Church Music, *In Tune With Heaven* chapter 30.

- [D.2] It is worth remembering that if a lot of your congregation are young or unused to church then even some of the old 'familiar' hymns will be just as unfamiliar to them as some of the newer songs.

- [D.3] Are you getting the balance right between using familiar material that enables the congregation to join in fully, and introducing new material to increase the repertoire? Are you introducing material which is appropriate to the ability of your choir/music group or congregation? Do you give the congregation any help with learning new material (settings or songs), for example, with a congregational practice? If there is conflict between musicians of different styles in your church it is worth considering whether the conflict is at root really about *style*, or whether it is not really a matter of mistrust. Often the

---

31 There is helpful material about symbolism in worship in Trevor Lloyd's, *Ceremonial in Worship* (Grove Worship series no. 75, now out of print).

underlying problem is that the organist just doesn't believe that the music group leader understands or is interested in offering God the very *best* quality music that we can; and the group leader may not trust that the organist really understands about worship which is Spirit led.[32] This can also apply between clergy and musicians!

SECTION E (Sermon, readings and prayers)

- In this section try not to get too bogged down in the details of the style of the particular preacher/prayer/reader on the days the questionnaire was used, or after which you had discussion. Concentrate on what could be done organisationally to help. Have you got facilities like an overhead projector (or other visual aids) easily available? Are there Bibles or ASBs in the pews (or available in church) for people to follow the readings if they would like to? Are the references given in full (either verbally or in notice sheet or on boards) for those who like to follow, and is there time for them to turn to the place? If you print a weekly service/notice sheet would it help to print out the readings (or at least the one to be preached from) or perhaps the collect? Is the preaching style appropriate to the type of service (whether it be choral mattins, all-age worship, or sung eucharist)?

- [E.5] The use of silence. This is a crucial issue, as many people have little chance for silence at home. And yet if there is a chance for a prolonged period of silence in church worship, they do not know what to do with it, and so get fidgety. What could you do to help people know about ways of using silence in corporate worship?

- [E.8] Is anyone feeling left out because they are young or old, or newcomers, or single or childless, or a different social background or race to the majority?

SECTION F (optional questions)

- [F.1] Reverence. People often have assumptions about what reverence means, often associating it with being solemn and quiet. As well as making people think, this question may help the team to understand the reasons behind some of the answers given to the other questions. The team may need to spend some time discussing this issue themselves as well as asking what other things are important in worship as well as reverence.

- [F.2] Other worshippers. Thinking of other worshippers is the first stage of acknowledging that corporate worship means more than lots of individuals offering individual worship at the same time and in the same place.

- [F.3] Private devotions at home. Many people come to church wanting to make their private devotions, and are therefore understandably disturbed when they are expected to acknowledge the presence of others, such as at the Peace. For many this is because they are unable (for all sorts of reasons) to worship at

---

32 John Leach has written helpfully on *Hymns and Spiritual Songs: the use of traditional and modern in worship* (Grove Worship Series no. 132).

home, or because no-one has ever shown them how to pray or read the Bible by themselves. Often there is then a clash of interests between those who need space for private devotion and those who need the corporate sense of meeting together to offer worship.

- This may reveal a need for education and pastoral follow-up. It may also reveal a need to look at issues like the use made of the Church building during the week for quiet prayer, the Daily Office, other mid-week services, and the designation of some service or part of a service on Sunday for quiet personal worship and prayer (something which is often happening by default). You may also like to consider other ways of helping people link their Sunday praying together with their weekday praying alone or in families.
- One thing that people in the past found helpful for their private prayers was a familiarity with memorable parts of public prayer (e.g. the Lord's Prayer, and the Collects).[33] Is your public worship regularly incorporating memorable prayers which could help people with their own prayers at home?

---

33 See Graham Pigott's, *Prayers to Remember* (Grove Spirituality Series no. 52) for a discussion of the value of committing key prayers to memory, and a selection of such prayers with discussion material for people to use in small groups.